A BUSINESS APPROACH TO CUCUMBER FARMING

Complete Entrepreneurial Step By Step Guide To Cucumber Garden From Scratch

ZHURI HART

DISCLAIMER

This book is intended to provide general information and insights on adopting a business approach to farming. The content within is based on the author's knowledge and experiences up to the date of publication. It is essential to recognize that the field of agriculture is dynamic, influenced by various factors such as market conditions, climate, and regulatory changes.

Readers are advised to conduct thorough research, seek professional advice, and consider their unique circumstances before implementing any strategies or practices discussed in this book. The author and publisher disclaim any responsibility for the accuracy, completeness, or suitability of the information provided. The book is not a substitute for professional advice, and the author and publisher shall not be liable for any damages or losses arising from the use or reliance on the information presented herein.

Individual results may vary, and success in farming enterprises is contingent upon numerous variables. The author encourages readers to consult with relevant experts, agricultural extension services, and legal or financial professionals to tailor strategies to their specific needs and local conditions.

This book is not intended to be a comprehensive guide to all aspects of farming, and readers should exercise their judgment and discretion in applying the principles discussed. The author and publisher do not endorse any specific products, services, or companies mentioned in this book unless explicitly stated.

By reading this book, the reader acknowledges and accepts the inherent uncertainties in agricultural endeavors and agrees to use the information at their own risk.

TABLE OF CONTENTS

ABOUT THE BOOK

This book, "A Business Approach to Cucumber Farming," provides a thorough and analytical framework for anyone hoping to take a more business-minded and strategic approach to growing cucumbers. The introduction part gives a basic overview of the cucumber farming sector while highlighting how important it is to use a business strategy to ensure sustainability and long-term success.

The book covers the basic principles of cultivating cucumbers, including which kind to cultivate, how to grow them, and how long cucumber plants take to mature. This information serves as the foundation for the portions that follow, especially the crucial "Market Analysis" chapter.

Readers obtain a thorough grasp of market dynamics from this section, including trends in supply and demand, competition analysis, and the recognition of possibilities and obstacles in the market. These kinds of information come in very handy when making decisions that have a big impact on how profitable a cucumber growing operation is.

"Business Planning," emphasizes the value of having specific goals and objectives. Along with financial predictions and budgeting, thorough guidance on creating a business plan gives readers the skills they need to launch a successful and long-lasting cucumber farming operation.

Important topics like crop management, post-harvest handling and harvesting, and farm infrastructure and equipment are covered. Farmers can use these sections as a reference for making strategic decisions about the site, crop techniques, and necessary equipment. Comprehending the best planting methods, and irrigation plans, and controlling pests and diseases are essential for establishing a strong base for cucumber cultivation.

The book goes on to highlight the importance of successful marketing strategies in "Marketing Strategies."

This section is an essential tool for making sure that the cucumbers grown are efficiently sold, covering everything from online and offline marketing tactics to relationship-building with buyers and branding.

"Sustainable Practices" highlights how important ecologically friendly farming practices are becoming. This chapter examines the growing need for sustainable agricultural techniques with an emphasis on organic cucumber farming, environmental protection, and adherence to certification and compliance criteria.

The crucial topic of "Financial Management" is finally covered. Through guidance on accounting, profitability analysis, and record-keeping, the book gives readers the financial literacy needed to successfully manage operating costs and overall business sustainability.

"A Business Approach to Cucumber Farming" is essentially an extensive manual that goes beyond conventional farming literature.

CHAPTER ONE

CUCUMBER FARMING INTRODUCTION

AN OVERVIEW OF THE INDUSTRY FOR CUCUMBER FARMING

A vital component of the agricultural landscape, the cucumber growing sector adds considerably to the world's fresh vegetable supply. As members of the gourd family, cucumbers are grown for their many culinary applications, such as salads and pickles, which has led to their widespread use in many different types of cuisine around the world. The sector reflects the versatility and adaptability of cucumber production by utilizing a range of cultivation methods, from sophisticated greenhouse practices to traditional open-field farming.

The growing demand from consumers for fresh food that is supplied locally has led to considerable development in the cucumber farming industry in recent years.

This tendency corresponds with the increasing focus on eating a nutritious diet and using sustainable farming methods.

Cucumber farmers and entrepreneurs are always looking for new ways to increase productivity, lessen their impact on the environment, and satisfy the growing demand from the market. Two such methods are hydroponics and vertical farming.

THE VALUE OF A BUSINESS STRATEGY

In the ever-changing world of agriculture, using a business strategy is critical to the long-term prosperity of stakeholders and cucumber growers.

The value of approaching cucumber farming from a business perspective goes beyond simple cultivation and includes several other aspects, such as supply chain management, financial planning, and market analysis. Farmers may effectively negotiate the hurdles presented by volatile markets, unpredictable climates, and changing consumer preferences by employing a strategic business approach.

Cucumber growers must also comprehend customer behavior and market dynamics to properly position their products. To increase their competitiveness in the market, farmers are encouraged by a business-oriented viewpoint to adopt best practices in crop management, make investments in cutting-edge technology, and form strategic alliances. This strategy plays a key role in guaranteeing the general sustainability of the sector as well as the financial sustainability of cucumber farming operations.

The value of the cucumber agricultural sector extends beyond its financial gains. It is essential to rural development because it creates jobs and sustains the livelihoods of many people who are involved in different phases of the supply chain. Additionally, by supplying a consistent and varied supply of cucumbers—which are abundant in vital minerals, vitamins, and antioxidants—the sector helps to ensure food security.

The world's agricultural sector includes the active and essential cucumber growing industry. Its importance is not limited to growing a well-liked crop; it also has social, economic, and environmental implications. Developing a business strategy is essential for managing the market's intricacies, guaranteeing sustainable operations, and supporting the expansion and success of cucumber farming businesses.

CHAPTER TWO

KNOWING ABOUT CUCUMBERS

DIFFERENT CUCUMBER TYPES

Cucumbers, or Cucumis sativus as they are formally called, are a versatile and refreshing vegetable that is a member of the Cucurbitaceae family of gourds. They are available in several types, each with special qualities and culinary applications. Slicing cucumbers are among the most popular varieties, and they're usually eaten raw in salads or sandwiches. Contrarily, pickling cucumbers are smaller and have a harder texture, which makes them perfect for pickling procedures. Because of their low seed count and mild flavor, specialty types of cucumbers, such as English or seedless cucumbers, are also very popular.

CONDITIONS AND NEEDS FOR GROWTH

Cucumber cultivation is dependent on certain growing conditions and requirements. Rich in nutrients and having a pH range of slightly acidic to neutral, well-drained soil is ideal for cucumber growth. For them to grow properly, they need enough sunlight, usually 6 to 8 hours a day in direct sunlight. The range of ideal temperatures is from 21 to 29 degrees Celsius (70 to 85 degrees Fahrenheit). To provide appropriate air circulation and avoid infections, plants must be spaced enough apart from one another. It takes regular irrigation to keep the soil consistently moist, especially throughout the flowering and fruiting seasons.

THE CUCUMBER PLANT'S LIFE CYCLE

Cucumber plants go through several stages in their life cycle, beginning with seed germination. Usually, cucumber seeds are planted immediately in the ground or started indoors before being moved. In ideal circumstances, germination takes place in 7–14 days. The seedlings grow into vines that bear both male and female flowers after they have germinated. Because of their monoecious reproductive system, cucumber plants can produce both male and female flowers. Fruit development depends on pollination, which is frequently made possible by bees or other pollinators.

Cucumbers grow from the ovaries of the female flowers following successful pollination. The fruit grows in stages, beginning as a little cucumber and progressively getting bigger as it ripens. Harvesting regularly is essential to promote ongoing fruit production. As annuals, cucumber plants go through their whole life cycle in just one growing season. The plant senses as the growth season draws to a close, which lowers the yield of cucumbers. Gardeners and farmers must comprehend the cucumber plant life cycle to maximize cultivation techniques and guarantee a plentiful yield.

CHAPTER THREE

EXAMINATION OF THE MARKET

DEMAND AND SUPPLY PATTERNS

For firms looking to make well-informed decisions, it is critical to comprehend demand and supply patterns in market analysis. The amount of a good or service that people are willing and able to buy at a specific price and time is referred to as demand. Conversely, supply denotes the amount of that good or service that manufacturers are prepared to put on the market. Evaluating customer preferences, economic conditions, and outside variables that may affect purchasing patterns are all necessary steps in the analysis of these trends.

Monitoring the fluctuations in supply and demand enables companies to forecast market conditions, modify their production schedules, and enhance their pricing tactics.

COMPETITOR ANALYSIS

Offering insights into the advantages and disadvantages of competing companies, competitor analysis is an essential part of market research. This procedure includes assessing the tactics, market share, and output of rival companies in the sector.

Through a thorough analysis of their offerings, cost models, routes of distribution, and promotional strategies, businesses can spot chances to set themselves apart and secure a competitive edge. Recognizing the actions of competitors also aids in forecasting changes in the market and creating successful counterstrategies.

To help firms remain adaptable in ever-changing marketplaces, this research takes into account not just immediate competitors but also possible new entrants, replacement products, and the competitive landscape as a whole.

MARKET OPPORTUNITIES AND PROBLEMS

Strategic planning and long-term success depend on the identification of market opportunities and problems. Opportunities come from gaps in the market, changing customer demands, new developments in technology, or adjustments in regulations.

Businesses can take advantage of these opportunities by developing new products, breaking into untapped markets, or improving current services. But opportunities can bring obstacles, which could include heightened competition, shifting customer tastes, or economic downturns.

Risk management and maintaining long-term viability depend on evaluating and reducing these obstacles. Proactively tackling obstacles and seizing opportunities are two traits of prosperous businesses that help them remain resilient in the face of unpredictability.

A thorough market study entails the identification of opportunities and problems as well as a deep grasp of supply and demand patterns and competitive dynamics. Businesses may create winning strategies, hone their value propositions, and negotiate the intricacies of the market environment by exploring these facets.

CHAPTER FOUR

PLANNING A BUSINESS

CLEARLY DEFINING YOUR OBJECTIVES AND GOALS

One of the most important steps in the company planning process is establishing specific goals and objectives. These objectives act as a road map, giving the company a defined course and assisting in directing the efforts of all parties involved in the pursuit of a single objective. Making sure your goals are SMART—specific, measurable, attainable, relevant, and time-bound—is essential when setting them. This framework aids in the creation of goals that are practical, attainable, and explicit within a specified time range.

CREATING A BUSINESS STRATEGY

Creating a thorough business plan is essential when it comes to business planning. A business plan serves as a strategic guide that describes the goals, vision, and mission of the company. It acts as a guide for the company, outlining important components such as the target market, competitive environment, marketing strategy, operational plan, and financial predictions in addition to the product or service offers. A well-written business plan is a useful tool for luring partners, investors, and other stakeholders in addition to offering advice to the company owner.

FINANCIAL PROJECTIONS AND BUDGETING

A key element of business planning is budgeting and financial projections, which are essential to the organization's sustainability and financial health. To accomplish particular objectives, budgeting entails allocating resources—both financial and non-financial—to different areas of the company. It supports limiting expenditure, controlling cash flow, and guaranteeing effective use of resources. On the other hand, financial forecasts entail making predictions about future financial performance using past data and current market patterns. Projecting income, costs, earnings, and cash flow helps to paint a realistic picture of the company's financial sustainability.

Accurate financial projections and a well-planned budget support risk mitigation, well-informed decision-making, and the general performance of the company. It enables the management group to recognize possible obstacles, strategically distribute resources, and adjust to shifting market dynamics. Furthermore, as it indicates a deep comprehension of the company's financial dynamics and a dedication to responsible financial management, having a strong financial plan is critical for drawing investors and obtaining funding.

Defining specific goals and objectives gives the company direction and a feeling of purpose, which helps to coordinate efforts and drive decision-making. To ensure that every part of the firm is taken into account and to articulate the strategic goal, a thorough business plan must be developed.

Ultimately, financial predictions and budgeting are essential tools for efficient resource management and for giving a realistic evaluation of the financial situation and prospects of the company. All of these ideas work together to create a solid business planning process, which is necessary for any organization to succeed in the long run.

CHAPTER FIVE

INFRASTRUCTURE AND EQUIPMENT FOR FARMS

SELECTING THE IDEAL SITE

A farm's success can be greatly impacted by its location, making it an important decision. A site's potential for agriculture is mostly determined by factors including soil quality, climate, availability of water, and market proximity. Testing of the soil is frequently done to determine the composition and amount of nutrients present, giving farmers insight into the potential for crop growth.

Examining temperature, precipitation trends, and frost dates are all part of the climate factors, which make sure the site is suitable for the crops being grown. Throughout the growing season, sufficient water sources—whether from irrigation systems or natural rainfall—are necessary to support crop development.

The cost of transportation and the effectiveness of customer access are other factors influenced by a market's proximity.

OPEN FIELD VS. GREENHOUSE CULTIVATION

There are two different agricultural methods: open-field agriculture and greenhouse farming, both having pros and cons. With the regulated environment that greenhouses offer, farmers may adjust the light, humidity, and temperature to produce the best growing conditions for plants.

Year-round cultivation and protection from unfavorable weather conditions are made possible by this regulated environment. However, building and maintaining a greenhouse can be expensive and need a large upfront payment. Conversely, open-field farming is dependent on inherent environmental circumstances. In terms of infrastructure, it is less expensive, but it is subject to seasonal restrictions and weather fluctuations.

Based on the particular crops, the environment, and other factors, farmers must carefully assess the advantages and disadvantages of each strategy.

CRUCIAL AGRICULTURE IMPLEMENTS

A vital piece of farming equipment is necessary for effective and successful agricultural operations. Common mechanical instruments for preparing soil, loosening compacted soil, and preparing appropriate seedbeds are tractors, plows, and tillers. Planting efficiency is maximized by using planters and seeders to help disperse seeds uniformly throughout fields. Sprinkler or drip irrigation systems provide a steady supply of water, especially in areas with erratic rainfall patterns.

Harvesting machinery, such as harvesters and combines, makes gathering crops more effective. Post-harvest machinery such as grain dryers and storage facilities are also essential to sustaining the quality of collected produce. Modern agricultural technology, like GPS-guided tractors and automated equipment, significantly improves farming operations' accuracy and efficiency, which raises yields and lowers labor costs. In conclusion, critical factors for farmers hoping to attain sustainable and prosperous agricultural practices include the careful selection of the ideal farming location, the decision between greenhouse and open-field cultivation, and the utilization of necessary farming equipment.

CHAPTER SIX

MANAGEMENT OF CROPS

PLANTING AND NURTURING SEEDLINGS

Given that they establish the groundwork for a productive crop cycle, planting and caring for seedlings are essential elements of successful crop management. First, premium seeds are chosen and checked to make sure they have the right characteristics for maximum development and yield. Farmers need to take into account things like seed variety, disease susceptibility, and climate adaptability. Effective seed storage and handling play a major role in the planting phase's effectiveness.

Planting requires careful attention to detail once the seeds have been chosen. Planting technique, depth, and spacing are important considerations that have a direct impact on seed germination and subsequent plant growth. To guarantee ideal planting circumstances, farmers must take into account the unique needs of each crop. Furthermore, planting time is critical, matching the right environment and weather to encourage strong seedling emergence.

Following the planting process, seedling care concentrates on the initial phases of plant growth. During this time, access to enough food and water, as well as protection from inclement weather, are essential. Crop diversification involves using mulching and row covers, among other methods, to protect seedlings from pests and high temperatures. Frequent seedling health monitoring enables prompt action to address problems like nutrient deficits or pest infestations that may limit plant growth.

TECHNIQUES FOR IRRIGATION

A crucial component of crop management is efficient irrigation, which is essential for giving crops the moisture they need to grow to their full potential. The amount of water required by different crops varies, thus farmers need to use appropriate irrigation techniques based on soil type, climate, and crop stage. There are various irrigation techniques, each with pros and cons, including sprinkler systems, flood irrigation, and drip irrigation.

For example, drip irrigation minimizes water waste and lowers the risk of illness by providing water directly to the base of plants. Sprinkler systems provide a more even application of water to crops by dispersing it over them in a fashion akin to that of natural rainfall. Conversely, flood irrigation entails saturating the fields with water to guarantee uniform hydration; nonetheless, it necessitates cautious handling to avoid water logging.

To improve water efficiency, precision irrigation technology like soil moisture sensors and automated irrigation systems are being used more and more. With the use of this technology, farmers may optimize crop productivity by monitoring soil moisture levels and providing water precisely where and when it is needed.

MANAGEMENT OF PESTS AND DISEASES

Controlling pests and diseases is essential to agricultural production because it protects plants from hazards that could lower crop quality and output. Integrated Pest Management (IPM) is a comprehensive technique that integrates multiple tactics to manage pests and illnesses while reducing the negative effects on the environment. This strategy makes use of resistant crop types, chemical control, cultural methods, and biological control.

The use of natural predators or parasites to manage pest populations is known as biological control. This approach contributes to the general equilibrium of the ecosystem and is sustainable and beneficial to the environment.

Crop rotation and good field hygiene are examples of cultural practices that interrupt the life cycle of pests and illnesses and therefore lower their prevalence.

Using pesticides for chemical management is a popular strategy for managing illnesses and pests. To reduce the impact on beneficial creatures and prevent the emergence of pesticide-resistant strains, however, considerable thought must be given to this. Farmers must be aware of the possible effects on the environment and adhere to specified application rates and dates.

One proactive approach to managing pests and diseases is to use crop types resistant to particular pests or diseases. The goal of plant breeding projects is to create naturally resistant crop varieties, so using chemicals is less necessary. A successful harvest is ensured by routine monitoring and the early discovery of pest and disease outbreaks, which enable rapid action to avert potential crop loss.

CHAPTER SEVEN

HARVESTING AND HANDLING AFTER HARVEST

BEST HARVESTING PRACTICES

One of the most important phases of agriculture, harvesting has a direct effect on the amount and quality of the finished product. The type of crop being grown, weather and crop maturity are all important considerations for optimal harvesting strategies. Maximum yield and quality are guaranteed when harvesting at the proper stage of maturity. In the case of fruits and vegetables, this usually entails choosing a moment to harvest that maximizes flavor and nutritional value.

Due to its efficiency and speed, mechanized harvesting is becoming more and more common, especially in large-scale agriculture. Nonetheless, cautious calibration is necessary to prevent crop damage. However, hand harvesting is still a common practice for delicate crops or those with erratic ripening patterns. It is a traditional procedure. The crop in question, the volume of production, and the resources available all influence the harvesting technique selection.

POST-HARVEST STORAGE AND MANAGEMENT

Several procedures are included in post-harvest management to maintain the quality and extend the shelf life of harvested crops. This stage is essential for minimizing losses and guaranteeing that the goods are delivered to customers in the best possible shape. The activities of immediate post-harvest include packing, sorting, and cleaning. While sorting makes sure that only produce of the highest caliber is chosen for additional processing or market distribution, cleaning gets rid of dirt and trash. Crops that are packaged properly are shielded from contamination, temperature changes, and physical harm while being transported.

The preservation of the freshness of harvested crops is contingent upon storage conditions. The demands of temperature, humidity, and ventilation differ amongst crops. Cold storage facilities—like refrigeration and storage under a controlled atmosphere—are frequently utilized to impede the growth of germs and slow down the ripening process.

Technologies like modified atmosphere packaging also contribute to the creation of an environment where perishable goods' quality is preserved.

MEASURES FOR QUALITY CONTROL

At every level of the post-harvest and harvesting processes, quality control procedures are crucial to ensuring that the finished product fulfills the required criteria. Potential problems are found and fixed earlier when quality control procedures are followed and routine inspections are conducted.

Size, color, texture, flavor, and other characteristics are frequently evaluated to determine the overall quality of the product.

Additionally, monitoring for infections, pests, and physical damage is part of quality control. Integrated pest management techniques can be utilized to reduce pesticide usage while preserving crop health. Technology has grown more and more useful in automating the quality control process, enabling rapid and precise evaluations. This includes the use of sensors and imaging systems.

The accomplishment of ideal harvesting, efficient post-harvest management, and the use of strong quality control procedures are essential to the success of farming methods. All of these procedures help to reduce losses, preserve the quality of the product, and efficiently and sustainably meet customer expectations.

CHAPTER EIGHT

ADVERTISING TECHNIQUES

HOW TO BRAND YOUR CUCUMBERS

When it comes to marketing, branding matters for even the most basic goods, like cucumbers. It's not only about products and services, though. Cucumbers are branded by giving them a distinct identity that makes them stand out from their competitors. The brand name, logo, and packaging design can all effectively convey this identity. Developing a memorable brand for your cucumbers helps to create a sense of trust and quality linked with your product, in addition to helping to establish consumer identification.

When creating your brand narrative, take into account elements like the cucumber's origin, cultivation techniques, and any distinctive characteristics it may have. Cucumbers may go from being just another commodity in the market to desirable, distinctive products with a strong brand story.

DEVELOPING RELATIONSHIPS WITH CUSTOMERS

Building and maintaining relationships with customers is the foundation of effective marketing. This means that marketing cucumbers entails more than just a straightforward transaction. Understanding your target audience and interacting with them on a deeper level are necessary for relationship building.

This could entail undertaking projects like producing instructional materials about the health advantages of cucumbers, providing behind-the-scenes tours of the growing process, or incorporating customers in the selection process via questionnaires or other feedback channels.

You may build a relationship and sense of loyalty with your customers that extends beyond a single transaction by actively listening to them, attending to their requirements, and offering more value. In addition to improving customer satisfaction, this buyer-centric strategy lays the groundwork for sustained market success.

ONLINE AND OFFLINE MARKETING STRATEGIES

In the linked world of today, a thorough marketing plan harmoniously combines online and offline strategies. Like many other things, cucumbers may be found online, where a wealth of options is available. By creating a strong online presence with a specialized website and by utilizing social media channels, you can interact with prospective customers in real-time and reach a larger audience. Showcase your branded cucumbers with eye-catching content, and think about adding e-commerce features for direct sales.

Conversely, offline marketing strategies target conventional media.

This can entail joint ventures with nearby supermarkets, and farmers' markets, or even taking part in neighborhood activities. Using both offline and online tactics guarantees a comprehensive strategy that increases the reach of your cucumber marketing initiatives and caters to a variety of consumer preferences. These strategies work together to produce a comprehensive and successful marketing campaign that will help your cucumbers succeed in both online and offline sales channels.

ECO-FRIENDLY METHODS OF GROWING CUCUMBERS

An example of a sustainable agricultural method that places an emphasis on ecological balance and reduces the use of artificial inputs is organic cucumber growing. This technique does not employ synthetic fertilizers, pesticides, or herbicides; instead, it depends on natural processes to nourish and protect the crop. Using cover crops and adding organic matter to the soil is how organic cucumber farming aims to improve soil health. In addition to guaranteeing the production of pesticide-free, healthy cucumbers, this strategy supports the agricultural ecosystem's overall sustainability.

PROTECTING THE ENVIRONMENT IN AGRICULTURE

One of the most important components of sustainable agricultural practices is environmental conservation, which includes a variety of tactics meant to reduce the negative effects of farming operations on the environment.

Adopting agroecological principles, which support the integration of crop rotation, biodiversity, and ecological balance, is one essential element. Conservation tillage practices assist preserve soil structure and reduce soil erosion. Examples of these practices include limited tillage and no-till farming. Furthermore, effective irrigation practices, a decrease in greenhouse gas emissions, and conscientious use of water resources are essential components of agricultural environmental conservation. Farmers may support the preservation of natural habitats, soil fertility, and the general health of ecosystems by putting these methods into practice.

AUTHENTICATION AND ADHERENCE

For sustainable farming methods to be successful and credible, certification and compliance are essential. Farmers who want to be certified as organic or environmentally sustainable must follow requirements and criteria set by various organizations and regulatory bodies. These certifications attest to the fact that farmers are applying methods related to soil management, water use, and pest control that comply with established sustainability requirements. Adherence to these guidelines not only guarantees consumers that the products are sustainable, but also cultivates a responsible culture within the agriculture sector. Farmers support the larger objective of encouraging ecologically and socially responsible agricultural

Practices by fulfilling certification standards., organic cucumber farming, agricultural environmental conservation, and certification and compliance are all interrelated components of sustainable agricultural operations. An all-encompassing method of production that places an emphasis on ecological health and reduces dependency on artificial inputs is demonstrated by organic cucumber growing. In agriculture, environmental conservation refers to a variety of tactics that are used to reduce the negative effects that farming operations have on the environment while highlighting the importance of biodiversity, healthy soil, and resource efficiency. Consumers can feel confident about the ethical and environmental components of the products they buy when farmers follow sustainability standards that are set forth through certification and compliance. When combined, these ideas support a more resilient and sustainable agricultural system that honors the fragile equilibrium between human activity and the environment.

CHAPTER NINE

MONEY HANDLING

ACCOUNTING AND MAINTAINING RECORDS

The foundation of any organization's successful financial management is accounting and record-keeping. These procedures are necessary to keep an accurate and thorough record of the business's financial transactions, which serves as a strong basis for compliance and decision-making. The methodical recording of all financial transactions, including income, outlays, and investments, is known as record-keeping.

Businesses may monitor their financial health, spot patterns, and evaluate the effects of different financial decisions by keeping thorough records. Contrarily, accounting entails the interpretation and analysis of these data to provide insightful information that is useful for performance evaluation and strategic planning.

CONTROLLING OPERATING EXPENSES

A crucial component of financial management that directly affects a business's sustainability and profitability is cost management. The daily expenditures associated with operating the firm, including rent, wages, utilities, and raw supplies, are included in the term "operational costs." Achieving efficient cost management requires a careful balancing act between keeping operations running smoothly and making the most out of spending. Businesses use several tactics to control operating expenses, such as implementing cost-control measures, negotiating favorable contracts with suppliers, and adopting efficient operational processes. This proactive strategy promotes long-term viability and competitiveness while also protecting the company's financial health.

ANALYSIS OF PROFITABILITY

A crucial component of financial management, profitability analysis offers insights into the health and prosperity of a company's finances. Assessing the correlation between earnings and outlays is necessary to ascertain the total profitability of individual goods or services, as well as the enterprise as a whole. Organizations can improve overall financial performance by

identifying their most profitable businesses, allocating resources effectively, and making well-informed decisions by performing a complete profitability study. Numerous financial measures, including return on investment, net profit margin, and gross profit margin, may be included in this analysis to provide a thorough understanding of the company's financial health and possible areas for development.

Careful farming cost control of operations, thorough record-keeping and accounting procedures, and perceptive profitability analysis are all necessary for efficient financial management. Together, these ideas give organizations the ability to maximize resources, make well-informed decisions, and successfully negotiate the ever-changing world of financial obstacles. An organization's current stability is guaranteed by a well-organized and disciplined approach to financial management, which also lays the groundwork for long-term, steady growth and profitability.